MIND OF MONEY

Navigating Money Decisions

George Blount

nBalance Financial

CONTENTS

UNTITLED

INTRODUCTION

As a Financial Therapist and Behavioral Economist, I help individuals overcome financial fears and assist organizations in using this information to create wellness programs. This book bridges the gaps I noticed in the industry, providing a distinctive and personalized approach to financial services.

We are emerging from a pandemic during which many individuals limited their spending. As we adjust to pre- and post-pandemic behaviors, you should change some habits developed during this period.

If your spending is reactive to emotional situations or the environment, leading to uncontrolled urges, it might signal a need for further investigation. This book explores the mind of money and aims to help individuals overcome their financial fears.

MONEY HATES YOU

What you believed about money as a child has shaped your financial behavior, potentially harming your future prosperity. Our attitudes, beliefs, and behaviors towards money are formed in childhood and often carried into adulthood, affecting our financial well-being.

What does this mean?

In childhood, we respond emotionally to money events because we respond emotionally to everything at that age. Feelings of helplessness, exclusion, rejection, disrespect, jealousy, embarrassment, or disappointment related to money form the foundation of our financial mindset.

As adults, these emotions harden into fear, anger, or disgust towards money. These negative emotions become barriers to your prosperity.

Financial circumstances create a series of money wounds over time. Internally, you are at war, fighting battles that hurt and need healing.

Unconscious conditioning makes it difficult to attract money. However, once addressed, you can become magnetic to opportunities and wealth. The keys to financial freedom are healing your negative self-image related to money and rebuilding financial barriers over time.

Money doesn't like you, but I'm here to change that. The bottom line is that money "hates" most Americans. This isn't about banking, budgeting, retirement, jobs, or investments. Your money mindset repels financial guidance and advice. It is the root of the problem and the best place to start.

OVERCOMING MONEY FEARS

Many people experience money-related fear, so we must address this fear. Overcoming these fears can effectively remove financial barriers.

People often don't admit they're scared of money. Instead, they use words like "overwhelmed," "worthless," and "helpless." They dismiss opportunities, are skeptical of change, or feel numb. These words are branches on the tree of fear and anger; regardless of the words used, the underlying emotions are fear and anger.

Money should make you feel free, prosperous, confident, respected, thankful, hopeful, inspired, or creative. These are all branches of the tree of happiness, so we often think money will "make us happy."

To overcome fear, you must understand what you

fear. Unfortunately, most people struggle to articulate their money fears. Here are the most common ones.

What is Money Fear?

Money fear is a feeling of dread or nervousness, often about the future. It can also stem from thoughts about not having enough money to live as you want.

Fear influences all financial decisions, from the jobs we take or keep to our ability to save or not save.

We fear losing what we currently have, but we are also scared of taking risks to make more in the future.

Money fear can affect one's entire life, impacting physical and mental well-being and relationships.

Attitudes, beliefs, and actions toward money are developed when we are young. These become our financial behavior and, in most cases, create barriers to wealth building.

MONEY FEARS

Fear of the Unknown

You need to understand how your money works. Planning a healthy financial future is like training for a marathon. You need to know when to begin, how to train, plan the journey, and enjoy the experience.

You need to understand what happens on the journey to enjoy the process, but you will fail to reach the finish line.

Fear for Survival

You need more money to survive. Seven out of ten workers live paycheck to paycheck. You will experience a crisis if you don't have a plan.

What makes a life crisis worse is the stress of not having alternative solutions for financial problems.

This is why financial education is so important.

Making better decisions around what and how we earn and make money work for you.

If you are forward-thinking, you can prepare for any potential financial issues.

Fear of Failure

It would be best if you had a proven plan. A plan is what will drive you through the year.

With a plan, you will start.

It would be best if you created financial freedom with a plan.

Create ongoing tactics to save.

Set aside 10% of your income or save a certain amount every month towards something in the future.

The key to success is to learn ways to save money and produce passive income.

Wealth building is an 80% mindset. Working on the mental barriers that prevent wealth building is an excellent place to start.

Fear of Clarity

I call HOPE land a place where dreams about becoming financially free are fulfilled because hope says, "I can."

Hope says, "I can," but in reality, hope says, "I could" or "I will."

Hope places you in the middle of potential failure.

Your goal needs to be crystal clear and measurable.

Apply the SMART concept to your financial goals.

Fear of Asking for Help

You did not learn how to overcome financial fear.

Financial fears can hold you back from freedom. Most people do nothing about financial concerns because they are scared of change.

Are you ready to decide what needs to change to overcome financial fear?

Financial problems attach to other aspects of life.

The only way to get to the root of financial stress is to discuss your relationship with money.

Money-saving experts don't make a living by teaching people how to save. They make money by helping create financial wellness.

Your money mindset is holding you back.

No one can give you certainty, but life will teach you about affordability, risk, and reward.

BASIC MONEY DECISIONS

Human Needs

The foundational needs for food, water, and sleep must be met for individuals and, where applicable, their dependents.

This aligns with our earnings: the mode of employment, where we work, when we work, how much we make, and the result of working.

Let's assess career opportunities and how to get a new job or grow in your existing position.

Safety & Protection

The next level is safety and security and how safely we can satisfy our needs. This level aligns with housing and transportation costs.

How safe and secure is my home, neighborhood, or community for my family and me? Discuss your housing situation and whether it suits your mental and financial health.

Your Support

The next level focuses on relationships and friends or socializing and leisure activities.

Does cost or affordability impact your ability to socialize? Do you have the time or energy to engage in such activities?

More importantly, can you discuss financial matters with friends or partners?

Let's work to understand your financial story so that you can share and align with the economic stories of others.

Esteem and Self-Actualization

Esteem is a feeling of accomplishment. This feeling arises from achieving goals like savings.

Once people can save their excess income, they need financial products and services such as investments or insurance to protect and preserve capital.

When individuals reach self-actualization or the ability to reach their potential, entrepreneurial activities may likely create personal equity.

MONEY EXPECTATIONS

1. Do you know what money is?

Money is not just an object or material; it's a form of control. It affects how we think and act; sometimes, both work together or against us.

2. Do you use money to see your life?

Our thoughts affect our lives, so we use money as a tool to envision a positive and prosperous future. Dream big.

3. Do you see your financial situation as a goal, a problem, or both?

Viewing your financial success as a goal can make you feel fulfilled and accomplished. Viewing it as a problem can cause hardship and stress in life.

4. Do you know how to manage your money?

You don't need to be a millionaire to understand the importance of money. Time, money, and financial freedom are your life's three most essential things.

Utilize them wisely.

5. Do you like to pay bills?

Most people prefer to avoid paying bills. However, bills must be paid. Therefore, learn how to manage your money wisely to avoid high-cost debt.

6. Do you use the money to achieve your goals?

Many families and individuals live paycheck to paycheck and do not save enough for the future. Use your money wisely to avoid financial disasters. Be disciplined and manage your time and finances effectively to achieve economic success.

BUILD A NEW FOUNDATION

B ecause of financial education, we can adopt a financial behavior that best suits our needs. This helps bridge the gap between what we know and what we do to survive.

Set a Budget

The most important step is setting a budget. Many tools, such as Mint, are available online to help you. Write your monthly income and expenses on your calendar to help you track how well you manage your costs.

Plan to Pay Off Any Debt

If you have debt, plan when you want to finish paying it off. Be realistic about your goals. Are you saving for a dream vacation? College? Retirement? Understand how much a million dollars would provide for you.

Create Healthy Financial Habits

Breaking the cycle of spending can be difficult, but it is possible. You have to make the change.

Don't sacrifice your health for money. It is better to be broke and healthy than broke and unhealthy.

Identify the lifestyle that is most appropriate for your financial and mental wellness.

Do you want to retire and have people ask what you did? Choose a profession that you enjoy. You can make enough money to live a comfortable life if you love what you do.

Build an Emergency Fund

An emergency fund is essential for unexpected situations. You never know when emergencies will happen.

Why start with specific criteria for purchases? Because then you can save. When you save more money, you build a significant cash reserve. This reserve can cover emergencies and help build assets like rental properties, tax-free savings accounts, and income-producing real estate.

WEALTH BUILDING SECRETS

T he wealthy often do not advertise their best practices or financial behaviors. Here are a few tips from my years of experience.

Choose the Right City to Live In

Affordability dictates savings; in many cities, it can be difficult to save while simply living. Take advantage of remote work and seek an affordable location.

Learn as a Group

Find a group that wants to become wealthy and motivate each other. If you are not part of a group, start one.

Need to save money? No problem. Learn as much as you can about money. There are many free services available to help you learn about finance:

a. Read a book.

b. Listen to a podcast.

c. Attend a free financial seminar. Financial seminars are low-cost and can often be a turning point in your life. If your local institution offers them, attend one and see how it works.

Be Humble About Your Wealth and Value

Your goals may be worth less money than you think.

Debt Can Be a Tool

Learn how debt works and use it boldly. Stay calm about your finances. Develop a long-term perspective.

The goal is to future-proof your money. Regardless of your age, where you live, work, or future interests, the money you earn today will give you Financial Freedom.

SPENDING PLAN

Prioritize your spending and think long-term. As someone once said, "Don't dig a hole that is deeper than your longest mouse." Instead of setting monthly goals, set yearly goals and learn how to forecast your outcomes.

Want to avoid being in the red? The easiest way to make money is to learn how to save more. My SMART spending plan is an excellent way to get started.

SMART Spending Framework

- **Specific**: Does this purchase pertain to a new financial goal, or will it constrain an existing goal?
- **Measurable**: If using credit cards or debt, how long will it take to pay off, and what are the costs associated with delaying?
- **Actionable**: Will this action delay or prevent the financial goals you have in place?
- **Reasonable**: Do you need this item? There are "want" and "need" buys; distinguishing between the two

is crucial because we often prioritize things we want over what we need. The focus of reasonableness is on "wants"-based purchases.

- **Timely**: Can you delay this purchase for some time? Determine the best time frame to make your decision (e.g., a month vs. three months), and once established, use it consistently.

Answer these questions and develop a personal policy. For example, it's a hard NO if my purchase does not pertain to a new financial goal or constrains an existing one. This means the purchase needs to meet my specific criteria. Stay on target.

GOAL SETTING

U se the SMART method to ensure that financial goals are realistic and achievable and to build confidence in future goals.

1. Set a Goal

Use SMART goal setting to ensure your goal has a purpose, is achievable, and builds confidence in your future goals. Specificity is essential when setting a SMART goal. Strive for a Specific, Measurable, Attainable, Realistic, and Timely goal.

2. Set a Timeline

Take time to be as detailed as possible. A timeline helps set expectations. To achieve more clarity, create a timeline that aligns with reasonable outcomes. Think of a timeline that makes sense, given your life circumstances.

3. Track Your Progress

A goal without a progress plan is meaningless. Progress tracking will help you stay motivated and on track. Measuring your progress keeps you accountable for completing the goal. Use your SMART goal review and measurement process to track your progress. Stay motivated by tracking progress. Remember to reward and acknowledge accomplishments along the way.

4. Goal Review

It is essential to review your weekly, monthly, quarterly, or yearly progress. Goal review does two things. First, it keeps you motivated and on track to accomplish your goals. Second, it allows you to adjust your path.

5. Plan for the Worst

The best-laid plans often need to be revised—plan for the worst. Plan for unforeseen circumstances that may arise. Breakdowns in the plan are just unfortunate events that happen. Trust in the process and remember that obstacles and challenges are opportunities. Keep going even if you're not able to reach all of your goals.

ABOUT THE AUTHOR

I am a financial therapist and founder of nBalance Financial. I help individuals learn how to navigate economic change and financial stress.

I teach financial concepts to non-licensed individuals who want the same information as those in the financial services industry without the jargon and sales pitch.

My educational background includes Johnson & Wales University, where I received a Bachelor of Science in Management degree, and Walden University, where I received a Master of Business Administration and Doctor of Business Administration.